A Little Thai Cookbook

Terry Tan

ILLUSTRATED BY SHERRI TAY

Appletree Press

First published in 1991 by
The Appletree Press Ltd
The Old Potato Station
14 Howard Street South
Belfast BT7 1AP
Tel: (0) 28 90 243074
Fax: (0) 28 90 246756
E-mail: reception@appletree.ie
Web Site: www.appletree.ie

A catalogue record for this book is available
from the British Library.

A Little Thai Cookbook

ISBN 0-86281-273-9

9 8 7 6 5 4 3 2

Introduction

Thais are largely Indo-Chinese, with a Buddhist culture going back some 3000 years to Hindu roots when India began trading with China after the silk and spice routes opened. Thai cuisine is predominantly spicy with intriguing hints of aromatic and heady fresh herbs. Chinese elements generally pale into submission under the plethora of coriander, lemon grass, coconut, tamarind, galangal, chilies, limes, ginger, and garlic that characterize much of the cuisine. A mouth-watering array of fruits and vegetables grow lush in verdant Thailand. Fish and shellfish are abundant in the riverine deltas, rice fields, and coastal regions. Poultry and pork are favored and beef is also popular, though strict Buddhists prefer not to eat it. Seemingly complex, Thai cooking is actually simple once you have mastered the art of blending the different spices, adding the fragrant top notes, and garnishing with a flourish. Both fresh and dried Thai herbs and spices are now increasingly available in Western countries. As with most Oriental cuisines, the keynote in Thai food is dependent on personal taste and there is no exact measure for coconut or chilies. You hone your instinct with this rule of thumb whatever precise measurements are given. Follow whatever suits you, bearing in mind this dictum and your penchant for more or less fire and coconut milk – the two fundamentals in Thai cuisine.

A note on measures
Spoon measurements are level except where otherwise indicated. Seasonings can of course be adjusted according to taste. Recipes are for four.

3

The Thai Kitchen

Apart from a few esoteric items, most ingredients in Thai cuisine are now available, especially as Thai restaurants are springing up with frequency. With Bangkok being such a heady tourist spot – culinary and otherwise – travellers bring back spicy memories of their exotic sojourn. What better sense of *deja vu* than that felt in a Thai restaurant fragrant with *sanuk* or promise – a catchall word that means to enjoy without restriction!

Rice (Khao) Thai fragrant, a premium brand of rice. Long grain, Basmati and Patna are also suitable.

Glutinous or sticky Rice (Khao Niew) Starchy, used mainly for desserts. Must be soaked beforehand.

Fish Sauce (Nam Pla) Soy sauce infused with seafood flavour and ubiquitous in Thailand.

Shrimp Paste (Kapi) Strong paste or dry cakes of fermented shrimp, essential in most spice blends.

Dried Shrimps (Khung Haeng) Used mainly for flavouring in sauces.

Tamarind (Nam Som) Moist lemony paste of tamarind pods. Lime or lemon are decent substitute.

Palm Sugar (Nam Taan Puk) Sold as *jaggery* in Indian stores; a coconut-flavoured solid sugar used in desserts.

Rice Noodles (Kway Teow) Dry or fresh white noodles in different thicknesses.

Wheat Noodles (Ba Mee) Usually dry, yellow cakes that need to be boiled or blanched before use.

Herbs and Spices

Where a recipe calls for meat, seafood or vegetable curry powder or paste, any commercial brand is usable. What's important are the fresh herbs sold by specialist stores.

Galangal (Khaa) Also known as Siamese ginger. Like ordinary ginger but with pink stems. Never used raw.

Lime Leaves (Makrut) These are to Thais what bay leaves are to Italians. Guitar-shaped leaves with strong lime flavor ideal for most spicy dishes.

Limes Jamaica limes come closest to these.

Lemon Grass (Ta-krai) Grass-like roots. Use only 2 inches of the root end, ground into paste or bruised to perfume soups.

Shallots (Horm Lek) Small red-skinned onions with sweet flavor. In a spice blend, ordinary onions will do as well.

Coriander, fresh Now widely available. Use roots and stems to grind in spice blend for delicate curries.

Chilies (Prik) Red or green, fresh or dried, the basis for all Thai spicy dishes. Use according to taste.

Screwpine or Pandanus Leaf (Toey) Herbaceous plant with faintly vanilla flavor to perfume and color desserts and rice. Try specialist stores.

Sweet Basil (Horapha) Like a cross between mint and liqorice. An essential topping for seafood curries.

Sauces Fish and chili sauces are available in specialty and Chinese stores.

Mee Krob

Crispy Noodles with Crab Meat

Thai cuisine has no specific breakfast fare. It borrows liberally from a potpourri of dishes. Likely as not, it will be noodles or sometimes rice, but it is always zesty with some sharp, hot, or rich spice blend. This particular dish is distinctive in the way the noodles are puffed up in hot oil.

---

8 oz rice vermicelli

10 fl oz/300 ml/1½ cups vegetable oil
4 oz/100 g/½ cup beansprouts
8 oz/250 g/1 cup crab meat
2 stalks spring onions, cut into inch pieces
2 tbsp hot chilli or Tabasco sauce
2 cloves garlic, ground
2 tbsp fish sauce
1 tsp pepper
spring onions to garnish

Heat oil until smoking and fry vermicelli in handfuls. They will puff up immediately. Set aside and remove all but 4 tbsp of oil. Fry garlic and chilli for a minute on medium heat and add beansprouts, crab meat and seasoning. Stir to incorporate and turn off heat. Toss in vermicelli and spring onions and stir well. Serve with more sliced spring onions and strips of fresh red chilli. Most dried vermicelli (thin rice noodles) come in 16 oz/450 g packets and only need to be soaked if you are making a dish with sauce. Allow 2 oz dry weight per person.

Khao Pad

Pineapple Rice

Rice is fundamental to Thai cuisine – indeed to life itself – and is treated with the reverence not usually accorded to accompanying stodge in other cuisines. Served in a scooped-out half pineapple, it becomes the *piece de resistance* of a breakfast or a banquet. Thai fragrant rice is ideal, but long grain, Basmati or Patna rice will do nicely.

12 oz/350 g/1½ cups cold cooked rice
1 fresh pineapple, halved and scooped out
3 eggs, lightly beaten

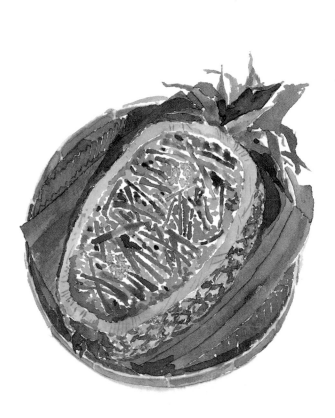

¾ cup raw shrimps
½ large onion, chopped
I fresh red chili, chopped
2 tbsp fish sauce
I vegetable stock cube, crumbled
5 tbsp vegetable oil
sprigs of coriander

Break up rice if lumpy. Chop pineapple meat and drain away liquid. Heat oil and pour egg in to make an omelette. When set, remove and slice into strips. Add a little more oil and fry chopped onion for a minute. Add shrimp, stock cube, fish sauce, rice, pineapple, and chili and stir over high heat for 2 minutes. Adjust seasoning with more fish sauce if necessary and ladle into scooped-out pineapple. Keep extras warm and top up. Garnish with fresh coriander and omelette strips.

Yam Neau

Little Salad

There's nothing diminutive about the flavor of this salad – the culinary term means much more than rabbit food in Thailand. Some Thai salads are state-of-the-art creations that include a dozen greens and fruits and mouth-watering dressings.

I ripe mango, peeled and sliced
I head endive (chicory)
2 leaves of the Chinese Leaf cabbage
I small unripe papaw (papaya) peeled and deseeded
I grapefruit, peeled and segmented
fresh coriander sprigs
Dressing
2 tbsp fish sauce

juice of 2 limes
1 tbsp sugar or 2 tbsp pineapple juice
1 clove garlic, chopped
2 tbsp nuts, finely chopped
3 tbsp warm water

Clean greens and fruits and slice into compatible shapes and longish slices. Arrange them in a spokeswheel pattern with chunky bits in the centre. Blend dressing and adjust to taste. Dribble all over salad just before serving and garnish with fresh coriander. Don't restrict yourself to exotic ingredients. It's the dressing that counts and even a tomato, lettuce and cucumber salad can become a Thai experience.

Kai Kwam

Pork and Prawn Omelette

You may think this an unlikely combination but Thai chefs have a way of making opposite culinary poles meet. The trick is to use spices to marry such different ingredients as pork and prawns – a union with delicious promise.

6 oz/150 g/½ cup minced pork	1½ tsp pepper
6 oz/150 g/½ cup cooked shrimp	pinch of nutmeg or mace
	2 tbsp fish sauce
1 tbsp fresh coriander, chopped	8 eggs, lightly beaten
	4 tbsp milk
3 tbsp coconut cream	5 tbsp oil
	chilli sauce

Heat 1 tbsp oil and gently cook minced pork and shrimp. Add coriander leaf, seasoning and coconut milk and stir until thick. Remove from heat. Add remaining oil to a clean pan and pour eggs in. Make sure your omelette pan is large enough to contain this

amount. Cook over low heat until egg is set at the bottom but still soft on top. Place filling on half of the omelette and gently flip over other half to form a half moon shape. Cook for 3 or 4 minutes more until outside is light brown and slightly crisp. Slide gently out of pan onto plate and when cool, slice and serve with a sharp chilli sauce. The traditional Moo Kwam is a difficult job of mashing cooked egg with the other ingredients and reshaping each for battering and deep-frying. This omelette innovation takes nothing away by way of taste.

Hor Mog

Spiced Fish in Banana Leaf

This dish, and the three following, are side dishes, but this is a misnomer, really, since Thai side dishes are often 'co-stars' that steal the thunder from main courses and make the meal. Whatever the blend of meat, seafood or vegetables and fresh herbs, each is a beguiling taste-teaser, never overpowering but complimenting every mouthful. Banana leaf is in short supply so use foil instead to make the same dish but without the tropical ambience.

---

8 oz/200 g/1 cup cod or halibut meat
1 tbsp fish sauce
1 tbsp lime juice
2 eggs
2 tbsp coconut cream
1 tbsp fresh ginger
2 red chillies
1 tsp ground turmeric
½ onion
1 stalk lemon grass (use 1½ ins/3½ cms of root end only)
1 tbsp ground coriander

Flake and mash fish meat to a fine paste. Blend or process with all other ingredients and ground spices. Place 2 tbsp of mixture on a 6 inch square of foil or banana leaf. Fold over sides and under again to make a firm parcel. Grill for 4 or 5 minutes, opening up foil or banana leaf at the last minute to slightly char the mixture. Serve with plain rice or bread and sliced cucumber and pineapple rings.

Chicken Satay

Sometimes spelled "Sate", this ubiquitous sliver of spicy flavor is indigenous to most of South Asia. Along every busy street in every Thai town or village, invariably there's a satay hawker offering succulent skewers of chicken, pork, beef, or prawns. And there are as many spicy variations as there are seeds in a papaya.

1½ lbs chicken breast	1 tbsp sugar
1 tbsp ground coriander	2 tbsp oil
1 tbsp ground cumin powder	1 tsp salt
1 tsp ground turmeric	12-20 bamboo skewers (yield
2 tbsp onion, finely chopped	depends on amount you
	skewer)

Slice chicken meat into 1 inch cubes. Marinate in spices and seasoning for at least half an hour. Skewer 3-5 pieces on each stick and shape to firm up. Grill in batches of 6 so you can handle them without trouble; about 3-4 minutes will do depending on distance from grill. For summer barbecues, grilled satay sticks on charcoal are an exotic treat.

Peanut Sauce
The traditional accompaniment to satay is peanut sauce, sliced cucumber, pineapple, and raw onion.

6 tbsp oil	1 tbsp shrimp paste (kapi)
2 large onions	1 tbsp sugar

3 red chillies	1 tsp salt
2 stalks lemon grass	1 tbsp tamarind paste
3 slices galangal (greater ginger	10 fl oz/300 ml/1 cup water
or Laos root) or ginger	6 oz/150 g ground peanuts

Grind onion, chillies, lemon grass, galangal or ginger, and shrimp paste to a paste. Fry in oil for 4 minutes and add sugar, salt, then peanuts and tamarind paste dissolved in water and strained. Simmer for a few minutes until oil rises to the surface. Remove and cool before serving.

Thom Yam Talay

Tamarind Seafood Soup

Thom Yam is to the Thais what whisky is to the Irish, a comparison that says it all for this most famous of Thai exports. The Thai saying goes that 'one will be sanctioned or condemned by one's Thom Yam'. Don't let this intimidate you for it's what you like that counts. The basis is a hot tamarind soup and the rest is plain ingenuity.

---

2 red chillies
2 cloves garlic
½ onion
3 tbsp oil
3 tbsp tamarind paste
20 fl oz/1 ltr/4 cups water
2 stalks lemon grass, bruised
2 red chillies, deseeded and sliced
2 tbsp fish sauce
½ tsp pepper
4 tiger prawns, peeled
1 large squid, sliced into rings

6 oz halibut, sliced

Blend first four ingredients and then fry the paste in oil until red and fragrant. Blend tamarind with water and strain. Place in a soup pot with fried paste and all seasoning ingredients. Simmer and add seafood to cook for 2 minutes. Adjust seasoning for taste and serve immediately. When frying Thom Yam paste, it is as well to make a large batch and refrigerate or freeze it for later use. Use sliced meat, poultry or vegetables as you please instead of fish for variations.

Moo Wan

Sweet Pork

This savory-sweet dish is often served as a topping for rice or noodles rather than as a dish on its own. It's delicious eaten, though, as a snack with a chili dip. Thais have a national habit of snacking all the time, any time!

1 lb lean pork, cut in two pieces
3 tbsp oil
2 tbsp sugar
3 tbsp dark soy sauce
4 cups water
2 tbsp palm sugar or brown (optional)

Heat oil and caramelize sugar until frothy and dark brown. Add pork and sizzle all over until sheen develops. Add water and simmer for an hour or longer till pork is fork tender. Add palm sugar or brown if you like it sweet. Remove pork to cool before slicing and serving with a chili dip. Try it as a sandwich filling.

Kaeng Khiu Wan

Green Prawn Curry

Thai meals are communal, with diners sharing from a central group of dishes served at once. There's always a hot curry, a crunchy salad and perhaps two or three side dishes to go with fluffy white rice. Thai curries are of three main types – red, yellow, green – the colours referring to chillies, turmeric, and fresh green herbs. The lesser-known Muslim curries proscribe the use of pork but are otherwise similar to red curries.

---

1 stalk lemon grass
3 slices galangal or ginger
2 green chillies, deseeded for milder flavour
1 tbsp dried shrimps, soaked till soft
½ onion
1 clove garlic
1 tbsp fresh coriander, chopped
1 lb/500 g raw peeled prawns
9 fl oz/300 ml/1½ cup coconut milk
1 tbsp fish sauce
1 tsp sugar
4 tbsp oil
1 tbsp lime juice

Blend first 7 ingredients, heat oil and fry the paste over medium heat until rich and fragrant. Add coconut milk, prawns and seasoning and simmer until prawns turn pink. The traditional Thai garnish is sweet basil which is rather like a cross between mint and aniseed, but you can use fresh coriander.

Normai Phad Moo

Pork with Bamboo Shoots

This is a versatile curry blend which marries well with any meat or even seafood. Bamboo shoots give it the distinctive flavor and crunch and they never loose the latter no matter how long you cook them. Use any canned variety, sliced or cubed.

4 dried red chilies, soaked until soft	I tsp shrimp paste (kapi)
½ onion	I tsp peppercorns
I tbsp dried shrimps, soaked until soft	I½ lb lean pork, sliced ¼ in thick and I¼ in square
2 cloves garlic	I cup sliced bamboo shoots
I stalk lemon grass	2 cups coconut milk
I tbsp sliced galangal or ginger	4 tbsp oil
I tsp ground turmeric	2 tbsp fish sauce
	I tsp sugar

Blend first 9 ingredients, heat oil, and fry paste until fragrant (about 3 minutes over medium heat). Add all other ingredients and simmer for 20 minutes until oil rises to the surface. Adjust seasoning and serve garnished with sprigs of sweet basil or fresh coriander. Unused bamboo shoots should be kept under cold water and can be refrigerated for up to a week. Change the water frequently.

Pla Nam

Whole Grilled Fish with Chilli Paste

Because they have such an abundance of sea and river fish, Thais elevate seafood cookery to an art form. For flavours closest to tropical fish, use halibut, mackerel, snapper, or large herring. And please leave the head on if you are serving it whole – it's sacrilege to decapitate any creature for it would not get through the pearly gates otherwise.

---

3 red chillies
3 cloves garlic
1 tbsp chopped ginger
3 lime leaves
1 whole tomato
1 tsp salt
1 tbsp sugar
2 stalks lemon grass
4 tbsp oil

Blend first 5 ingredients. Heat oil and fry paste over medium heat until aromatic. Add salt and sugar and a little water to make a thick sauce. Roughly shred 1 in/2 cms of the root end of lemon grass. Tie together to make a sort of basting brush. Spread paste all over fish, especially between scores. Heat grill and cook for 5 minutes on each side, using lemon grass to baste with oil. Serve with sliced cucumber or mango. If you cannot bear the beady-eyed look of whole fish use fillets or steaks. Symbolism aside, there is no difference in taste.

Kaeng Mussaman Gai

Muslim Chicken Curry

Though Thailand is largely Buddhist, there are many Muslims who live close to the Malaysian border. After centuries of cross culture, the two cuisines have influenced each other to a subtle or vigorous degree. Apart from the absence of pork, most Muslim dishes use the same basic ingredients.

---

2 tbsp ground coriander
1 tbsp ground cumin
1 tsp ground turmeric
1 tsp pepper
4 tbsp oil
1 large onion, chopped
1 tbsp grated ginger
2 tbsp tomato purée
1 whole chicken, about 2 lbs cut into bite-sized pieces
1 cup coconut milk
½ cup pineapple juice
2 tbsp fish sauce
2 tbsp lime juice
potatoes (optional)

Add water to ground spices and mix into paste (or use 5 tsps meat curry powder). Heat oil and fry onion and ginger until light brown. Add spice paste and tomato purée and fry over medium heat until oil separates. Add chicken pieces and stir so every piece is coated. Add coconut milk, pineapple juice, fish sauce, and lime juice and simmer for 25 minutes. For extra bulk, add peeled potatoes in the last 15 minutes. The finished dish should be a rich, red hue. Leftover curry gravy makes an excellent flavoring for curried fried rice.

Gai Yang

Spiced Grilled Chicken

Thai spices do not always raise the roof of your mouth. The absence of chili does not make it any the less delicious. Pepper is used often as a merely "warm" cousin and, in tandem with fresh herbs, can be as tantalizing as chili. The Thai penchant for using fresh coriander, roots and all, is pure culinary genius.

---

4 chicken thighs
4 cloves garlic
2 tbsp fresh coriander with root, chopped
1 tsp black peppercorns
1 tbsp fish sauce
2 tbsp lime juice
2 tsp sugar

Use whole chicken thighs on the bone. Make deep slits along the deepest parts. Blend garlic, coriander, and peppercorns to a fairly fine texture. Mix with fish sauce, sugar, and lime juice and rub deeply into chicken. Marinate at least an hour or even overnight. Grill for 10 minutes, turning over several times. To test if chicken is cooked through, poke a skewer into deepest part and, if juices run out clear, the pieces are done. Serve with chili, garlic, and vinegar sauce which is made by blending together 3 red chilies, 2 cloves of garlic, 2 tbsp vinegar, a pinch of salt, and 1 tsp sugar. A whole bird can be marinaded the same way, roasted for required length of time, then charred just a little under the grill.

Kaeng Gai Takrai

Chicken and Lemon Grass Curry

If you buy lemon grass, it is as well to get a lot of stalks and freeze them whole. Allow to defrost to room temperature before using. Remove one or two outer layers of root and use only 2 in/5 cms of it to fry in and perfume oil before adding spices. Discard when it turns brown.

1 stalk lemon grass	4 green chillies, deseeded and sliced
4 slices galangal	
6 candlenuts	6 shallots, sliced
1 tsp shrimp paste (kapi)	2 tbsp fish sauce
½ onion	1 tsp sugar
2 stalks lemon grass, sliced fine	1 tbsp lemon juice
	5 tbsp oil
4 lime leaves, sliced hair thin	4 chicken breasts, sliced
8 fl oz/250 ml/1 cup coconut milk	

Make a paste by blending the first 5 ingredients. Fry lemon grass and lime leaves with the paste until aromatic and add coconut milk and chicken. Simmer for 20 minutes until thick then add fish sauce, sugar and lemon juice. Heat oil and shallots until brown. Remove and set aside. Fry sliced green chillies and set aside. Serve garnished with fried shallots and green chillies. You can make sauce a day or two ahead and refrigerate; add chicken when required to save time when entertaining.

Kway Teow Nua Sap

Minced Beef Curried Noodles

This is a Chinese heritage spiced up. You can use any type of noodles if rice noodles are not available. Some Chinese and specialty stores sell fresh noodles which are excellent. This recipe uses the dried variety called rice sticks which, when soaked in hot water, become rice noodles.

---

12 oz rice sticks, soaked until soft
2 tbsp dark soy sauce
2 tbsp meat curry powder
1 tbsp minced garlic
8 oz minced beef
1 tbsp fish sauce
2 tbsp chopped spring onions
2 tsp cornstarch, blended with a little water
¾ cup water or beef stock
4 tbsp oil
fresh coriander and sliced chilies for garnish

Heat oil and fry drained noodles with soy sauce over high heat. Remove to serving plate. Fry garlic and curry powder in remaining oil, sprinkling a little liquid in to prevent burning. When well blended add beef, fish sauce, cornstarch, beef stock, and spring onions and cook until thick. Pour over noodles and serve garnished with fresh coriander and sliced chilies. Leftover cold roast beef, sliced thinly, makes an excellent substitute for minced beef and a few tablespoons of roast beef juices added to stock gives a richer flavor.

Pla Prio Wan

Ginger Fish

This is another hybrid with Chinese influence. The Thais sneak in enough chillies to wake the dead. Chinese cuisine, with the exception of Sichuan, does not use chilli at all. This calls for the freshest, meatiest whole fish because the skin crisps up nicely. Good salmon steaks do just as much justice to the sauce if you don't care for whole fish staring back at you.

---

4 salmon steaks
oil for deep frying
2 tbsp chopped ginger
1 tbsp preserved Chinese yellow beans
4 red chillies, sliced
4 Chinese mushrooms, soaked and sliced
2 stalks spring onions, sliced 2in/5 cms long
2 tbsp lime juice or vinegar
1 tbsp sugar
2 tbsp fish sauce
5 tbsp water

Clean fish steaks and deep fry until golden brown. Set aside and keep warm. Remove all but 3 tbsp oil and fry ginger until light brown. Add yellow beans, lightly mashed, and chillies and fry for 30 seconds. Add all other ingredients and when bubbling, taste and adjust seasoning before ladling onto fish steaks. The sauce can be thick or thin depending on your taste. Yellow beans come both whole and in paste form. The latter is more strongly flavoured.

Khao Pad Prik Kring

Fried Curried Rice

This basic accompaniment can be varied at will and transformed into a dish in itself by adding leftover meat or seafood. Always start with cooked, cold rice. The rest is sheer ingenuity, using this or that leftover curry paste or gravy. When cooking rice from scratch, rake through with a fork to loosen grains immediately after cooking. This will prevent lumps.

---

4 tbsp oil
½ onion, sliced
3 eggs, lightly beaten
2 tbsp curry paste or thick gravy
1½ cups cold rice
4 tbsp cooked shrimp
2 tbsp fish sauce
cucumber, sliced
fresh coriander

Break up rice to loosen grains. Heat oil and fry onion till soft. Put aside and cook egg till done. Cut up roughly and put aside. Add curry paste, rice, shrimp, and fish sauce and stir well over high heat for 2 minutes until well blended. Serve with sliced cucumber and fresh coriander. For buffet presentation, heap rice into a deep bowl and pat down firmly. Unmold on a large plate lined with fresh banana leaf and garnish with pineapple rings, sliced cucumber, and red pepper rings. This dish can be served as a main course accompaniment from smaller bowls with your main meat or seafood course.

Yam Yai

Great Salad

This salad is more than deserving of its grand name. It uses a plethora of tropical fruits and greens. Somehow, to use substitutes negates the whole purpose of Yam Yai so try to use all, or at least most, of the original ingredients. If you must, substitute green apple for mango, apricot or peach for star fruit, French or Kenyan beans for runner beans, and carrot for water chestnuts.

---

1 green mango
1 cucumber
1 star fruit (carambola)
4 long or runner beans, blanched for 2 minutes
4 cabbage leaves
1 small can water chestnuts
Sauce
4 tbsp fish sauce
1 tbsp chilli sauce
3 tbsp ground peanuts
2 tbsp lime juice
1 tbsp dried shrimps, soaked and pounded
1 tsp sugar

Wash green mango and slice thinly with skin. Remove cucumber pith and cut into 2 in/5 cm julien pieces. Remove ridges of starfruit and cut into $\frac{1}{2}$ in/1 cm thick star shapes. Cut runner beans into 2 in/5 cm lengths. Slice cabbage into $\frac{1}{4}$ in/$\frac{1}{2}$ cm strips. Leave whole or slice water chestnuts. Assemble on large plate and garnish with cucumber fans or tomato roses. Blend sauce ingredients and adjust to taste. Pour over salad or serve in a sauce boat.

Yam Nua Moo

Pork Salad

In the best tradition of stretching, when it comes to Thai meat salads, the result is rarely just mere substance. Compatibility of ingredients is the keynote here, and plain boiled pork is transformed into something quite tasty.

½ lb cold boiled lean pork, finely sliced
2 stalks spring onions, chopped
4 shallots, peeled and finely sliced
I small bunch mint, chopped
I green mango, peeled and chopped
½ cucumber with pith removed, diced
Dressing
I tbsp dried shrimps, soaked until soft
2 green chilies
I tsp shrimp paste, lightly toasted
2 shallots
I clove garlic
juice of 2 limes
I tsp sugar

Place salad ingredients in a large bowl and mix well. Blend dried shrimps, chilies, shrimp paste, shallots, and garlic to a paste. Mix with lime juice and sugar. Just before serving, toss well with salad ingredients and sprinkle with chopped nuts. Vary with cold beef, lamb, or even chicken for a summer salad.

Yam Pla Duk

River Fish Salad

This is definitive Thai cuisine. For this classic dish, the main ingredient is a local fish that must be pregnant with roe. However, any meaty fish combined with smoked cod's roe makes a more than satisfactory version. Palm sugar is also called *jaggery*. It is sold in solid form by most specialist Chinese and Indian stores. It has a distinctive coconut flavour and must be melted gently with a little water. Brown or demerara sugar can be used instead.

---

1 whole snapper
8 oz/130 g smoked fish roe
6 shallots, sliced
1 tbsp shredded ginger
1 tbsp lime juice
1 tbsp palm sugar
1 tbsp fish sauce
red chilli
fresh coriander

Clean and fillet snapper. Fry in hot oil until crisp and cut into bite-sized pieces. Mash roe and mix with all other ingredients. Arrange with cut-up fish pieces and garnish with strips of red chilli and fresh coriander. Serve with toast.

Nam Prik

Hot Shrimp Sauce

Sauces are not merely dips. Each is an important highlight to every Thai meal. Every one is an artful blend of sharp, hot, sweet, sour or salty flavours and also textures that you rarely get out of a supermarket bottle. Nam Prik is a national pride. Whether it's mouth-searing or simply warm depends on the amount of chillies. Thais use their favourite 'bird chillies' which are tiny infernos.

3 tbsp dried shrimps, soaked until soft	1 tbsp palm sugar
1 tsp shrimp paste (kapi), lightly toasted	3 tbsp lime juice
3 cloves garlic	2 tbsp fish sauce
3 red chillies	4 tbsp hot water
	1 tbsp coriander, finely chopped

Grind the first four ingredients to a paste and mix with the others. Taste and adjust. Serve in a sauce boat to go over cold meat, raw vegetable crudités, or fried seafood. As a salad sauce, add festive flair by putting sauce in scooped out halved cucumbers (lengthwise), or halved red peppers.

Nam Satay

Rich Peanut Sauce

Nearly as prolific as the satay it accompanies, this Thai peanut sauce is richer than all the other Southeast Asian versions because of the addition of coconut milk. Do not use peanut butter as a substitute for freshly ground peanuts if you can help it.

2 stalks lemon grass	1 cup water
4 slices galangal	3 tbsp lemon juice
6 dried chilies, soaked until soft	1 tbsp sugar
1 large onion	6 tbsp oil
2 tsp shrimp paste	2 tsp salt
3 cloves garlic	4 tbsp ground peanuts
1½ cups coconut milk	

Blend first 6 ingredients, heat oil and fry for 3 minutes until oil separates. Add all other ingredients except ground peanuts, and simmer for a few minutes. Add peanuts, adjust taste and remove to cool.

Nam Horapa

Sweet Basil Sauce

Sweet basil (*horapa*) is an aromatic tropical herb rather like mint and liquorice in flavour. Half-and-half mint and basil gets quite good results. This is a sharp, sweet, minty dip for seafood and meats.

½ large onion	3 tbsp lime juice
2 cloves garlic	1 tbsp melted palm sugar
2 tbsp sweet basil, chopped	1 tbsp sesame seeds
2 tbsp chopped nuts	fresh mint, chopped
4 red chillies, ground	

Chop the onion very fine and crush the garlic to get the oils out. Chop both together to blend. Mix with all other ingredients in a bowl and adjust taste. For a thicker sauce, add more chopped nuts and sesame seeds. Chill and garnish with whole sweet basil leaves or chopped mint. This sauce can also be used to coat grilled chicken, warmed through before serving.

Sangkhaya

Steamed Coconut and Egg Custard

For a party piece, this can be steamed in a hollowed-out pumpkin or in young coconut shells. Otherwise, a casserole dish will do nicely. Sankhaya is, in fact, a tropical jam eaten as is or with toast. Thais use only coconut milk squeezed from shelled and grated fresh nuts for puddings. Canned coconut milk will give you a more liquid consistency but is nonetheless rich.

---

1 cup thick coconut milk
½ cup granulated sugar
6 medium sized eggs
3 screwpine leaves (or 2 drops rose water)

Separate egg yolks and beat lightly. Add sugar and milk and stir until sugar dissolves completely. This is important or the custard will get lumpy. Screwpine leaves look rather like lily leaves and have a faintly vanilla flavor. Add them to mixture or use rose water, available at all Indian food stores, as a substitute. Strain the mixture through a fine sieve and steam for 1½ hours. Serve cold or warm.

Khanom Thuey

Coconut Cups

Thais have a particular penchant for diminutive desserts, and the smaller the desserts, the more Thais rise to the culinary challenge. Even street hawkers turn out rococo creations of little cakes and puddings shaped like tropical fruits in rainbow hues, many startlingly like the real thing. This simple but delicious recipe shouldn't give you too much of a challenge.

---

4 oz / 100 g / 1 cup rice flour
2 tbsp arrowroot
1 pt / 500 ml / 2 cups coconut milk
7 oz / 120 g / 1 cup palm sugar
10 fl oz / 250 ml / 1 cup water
1 pt / 500 ml / 2½ cups thick coconut milk
3 tbsp rice flour
pinch of salt

Mix 1 cup rice flour with arrowroot and coconut milk. Melt palm sugar with water and strain as there could be some grit. When cool, mix with rice flour and coconut milk. Pour half way up ramekins or cupcake containers and steam for 30 minutes. Blend thick coconut milk with 3 tbsp rice flour and salt and pour onto tops of steamed pudding. Cook until set and cool before unmoulding.

Tako Haew

Water Chestnut and Coconut Pudding

In the same genre as Khanom Thuey, these cups of creamy coconut and crunchy water chestnuts are an ambrosial blend of fragrance, flavor, smoothness, and crunch. Without screwpine or "toey" leaves, tako is merely blancmange. If you really want to go to town, soak jasmine blossoms in the water overnight and staple broad screwpine leaves into little cup shapes to serve the Tako.

---

10 canned water chestnuts, chopped
½ cup cornstarch
1 tbsp arrowroot
1 cup sugar
3 cups water
4 screwpine leaves
Topping
2 cups coconut cream
½ tsp salt
1 tbsp rice flour

Cut screwpine leaves into pieces and pound to extract color and fragrance. Combine with cornstarch, arrowroot, sugar and water, and cook over low heat until mixture is thick and clear. Add chopped water chestnuts and pour into shallow pie dish or small ramekins, Meanwhile, blend coconut cream, salt, and rice flour and cook quickly to thicken. Pour over water chestnut mixture and chill. If made in a shallow pie dish you can cut into squares or diamond shapes when chilled and set.

Kluey Buah Chee

Palm Sugar Bananas

Thai bananas come in dozens of shapes, colours and fragrances but even the ordinary bananas you buy in temperate countries become completely different when given a little *sanuk* or special treatment. This pudding can be served as is or with steamed, glutinous rice.

6-8 bananas, peeled and cut into chunks
4 tbsp melted palm sugar
2 tbsp granulated sugar
2 pt/1 ltr/4 cups water (less if you like it thick and rich)
2 screwpine leaves, tied into a knot (optional)

Simply combine all ingredients and simmer until bananas are just soft enough but not breaking apart. Chill thoroughly and serve cold or warm. If you want to make it as a topping for glutinous rice, reduce the water by half and make a thick version. To make the rice, soak about 4 oz/80 g/½ cup glutinous rice with water to an inch above rice level for 2 hours. Place in steamer or microwave and cook until dry and cooked through. Chill and serve with Kluey Buah Chee. For a festive meal, cut fresh banana leaf into rounds the size of dessert plates. Place 2 tbsp rice on them and top with Kluey Buah Chee.

Index